the *ultimate*
vegetarian
air fryer
cookbook

Stella Harper

LEGAL & DISCLAIMER

The information contained in this book and its contents is not designed to replace or take the place of any form of medical or professional advice; and is not meant to replace the need for independent medical, financial, legal, or other professional advice or services, as may be required. The content and information in this book has been provided for educational and entertainment purposes only.

The content and information contained in this book has been compiled from sources deemed reliable, and it is accurate to the best of the Author's knowledge, information, and belief. However, the Author cannot guarantee its accuracy and validity and cannot be held liable for any errors and/or omissions. Further, changes are periodically made to this book as and when needed. Where appropriate and/or necessary, you must consult a professional (including but not limited to your doctor, attorney, financial advisor, or such other professional advisor) before using any of the suggested remedies, techniques, or information in this book.

Upon using the contents and information contained in this book, you agree to hold harmless the Author from and against any damages, costs, and expenses, including any legal fees potentially resulting from the application of any of the information provided by this book. This disclaimer applies to any loss, damages or injury caused by the use and application, whether directly or indirectly, of any advice or information presented, whether for breach of contract, tort, negligence, personal injury, criminal intent, or under any other cause of action. You agree to accept all risks of using the information presented inside this book.

You agree that by continuing to read this book, where appropriate and/or necessary, you shall consult a professional (including but not limited to your doctor, attorney, or financial advisor or such other advisor as needed) before using any of the suggested remedies, techniques, or information in this book.

TABLE OF CONTENTS

DESCRIPTION

Are you ready to embark on a journey of culinary delight while embracing the nourishing benefits of a vegetarian lifestyle? Look no further than our comprehensive guide, «The Ultimate Vegetarian Air Fryer Cookbook,» designed to inspire and tantalize your taste buds with a diverse array of delectable recipes. Within the pages of this book, we invite you to explore the vibrant world of vegetarian cuisine, where flavor and nutrition harmonize in perfect balance. Delve into the foundational chapters that delve into the principles of vegetarianism, its profound impact on health, and an array of recommended foods. Gain valuable insights into nutrition basics and expert tips for selecting the finest ingredients to elevate your culinary creations to new heights.

But that's just the beginning. Prepare to embark on an exciting culinary adventure as we introduce you to the revolutionary world of Air Frying.

Discover the inner workings and unparalleled advantages of this remarkable device, tailored specifically for crafting mouthwatering vegetarian dishes. From essential techniques to optimal usage tips, you'll uncover the secrets to mastering your Air Fryer and unlocking its full culinary potential.

Yet, at the heart of it all lies the irresistible allure of our healthy recipes. From tantalizing snacks and refreshing salads to hearty mains and decadent oil-free desserts, each dish is crafted with precision and passion to cater to every vegetarian palate. With the assistance of your Air Fryer, you'll effortlessly whip up nutritious and flavorful meals that will leave you craving more, day after day. «The Ultimate Vegetarian Air Fryer Cookbook» transcends the realm of a mere recipe collection. It serves as a holistic guide to embracing a wholesome lifestyle, showcasing the ease and deliciousness of vegetarian cooking using modern culinary techniques. Immerse yourself in the boundless possibilities of vegetarian cuisine and elevate your dining experience to new heights with this inspiring and indispensable book.

VEGGIE DELIGHTS: HEALTHY COOKING FUNDAMENTALS

Venturing into the realm of vegetarian cuisine unveils a vast expanse of culinary delights, where an array of flavors, textures, and aromas converge to create a symphony for the senses. Here, amidst a cornucopia of plant-based ingredients, we discover not merely a dietary preference, but a profound philosophy that resonates with both personal wellness and environmental stewardship.

Vegetarian cuisine transcends the confines of mere sustenance; it embodies a rich tapestry of cultural traditions, culinary ingenuity, and nutritional wisdom. From vibrant salads bursting with freshness to hearty stews simmering with wholesome goodness, each dish tells a story of vitality and nourishment.

But beyond its gastronomic allure, vegetarianism is a holistic approach to living that promotes harmony with the natural world. By eschewing animal products in favor of plant-based alternatives, we embrace a lifestyle that not only benefits our own health but also fosters ecological balance and sustainability for generations to come.

In essence, vegetarian cuisine beckons us to embark on a journey of culinary exploration and self-discovery. It invites us to savor the abundance of the earth's bounty and to cultivate a deeper appreciation for the interconnectedness of all living beings.

Foundations of Vegetarian Cuisine

At the core of vegetarian cuisine lies the principle of using plant-based products as the primary source of nutrition. Fruits, vegetables, grains, legumes, nuts, and seeds form the foundation of the diet, providing the body with all necessary nutrients.

Creativity and variety play a pivotal role in vegetarian cooking. Combining different ingredients, utilizing spices and seasonings, as well as employing various cooking methods allow for the creation of impressive dishes that delight both the palate and the eyes.

Benefits of Vegetarian Cuisine

Health Improvement:
The vegetarian diet is associated with numerous health benefits. It helps reduce the risk of cardiovascular diseases, diabetes, obesity, and certain types of cancer. Moreover, the vegetarian diet is typically rich in antioxidants, vitamins, and minerals essential for maintaining health and well-being.

Environmental Sustainability:
Transitioning to a vegetarian diet contributes to reducing the negative impact on the environment. The production of plant-based food requires less land, water, and energy, and generates fewer greenhouse gas emissions compared to animal product production.

Ethical Considerations:
Many individuals choose a vegetarian diet due to ethical reasons, aiming to protect animal rights and alleviate the suffering associated with their use in the food industry. Vegetarian cuisine allows satisfying the body's needs without harm to animals.

Diversity and Creativity:
Vegetarian cuisine offers a vast array of ingredients and dishes capable of satisfying any taste preferences. From light salads and soups to hearty main courses and delicious desserts, vegetarian cuisine inspires culinary experiments and new discoveries.

Vegetarian cuisine is not just a choice for health and ecology but an opportunity to explore new flavors and experiences. The next step will be to explore recommended products and their nutritional properties.

Principles of the Vegetarian Diet

The vegetarian diet is centered around the consumption of plant-based foods while excluding meat and animal-derived products. It encompasses a wide variety of food groups, ensuring the body receives all essential nutrients. Here are the core principles of the vegetarian diet:

Fruits and Vegetables: Fruits and vegetables form the foundation of the vegetarian diet. Rich in vitamins, minerals, and antioxidants, they promote overall health and well-being. It's recommended to include a diverse range of fruits and vegetables in your diet to reap maximum benefits.

Grains and Grain Products: Grains such as oats, rice, wheat, barley, and corn are essential sources of carbohydrates and fiber in the vegetarian diet. They serve as the basis for many dishes and provide the body with sustained energy throughout the day.

Legumes and Soy Products: Legumes, including beans, lentils, chickpeas, and soy products like tofu and soy milk, are vital sources of protein and other nutrients for vegetarians. They offer an excellent alternative to meat and contribute to a balanced diet.

Nuts, Seeds, and Plant Oils: Nuts and seeds are rich in healthy fats, protein, vitamins, and minerals. Incorporating them into the diet provides essential nutrients and adds flavor and texture to meals. Plant oils such as olive oil, coconut oil, and avocado oil are sources of healthy fats and enhance the taste of dishes.

Dairy and Eggs (Optional): Some vegetarians choose to include dairy products and eggs in their diet as additional sources of protein and nutrients. However, this is not mandatory, and vegetarians can create nutritious meals without them.

The Significance of Healthy Eating and Choosing the Right Foods

Healthy eating is fundamental to overall health and well-being, providing essential nutrients that support bodily functions, maintain optimal health, and reduce the risk of chronic diseases. Making informed choices about the foods we consume plays a crucial role in promoting health and vitality. Here's why healthy eating and selecting the right foods are so important:

Nutrient Intake:
Consuming a balanced diet rich in fruits, vegetables, whole grains, lean proteins, and healthy fats ensures adequate intake of essential nutrients such as vitamins, minerals, protein, fiber, and antioxidants. These nutrients are vital for supporting immune function, promoting tissue repair, maintaining healthy bones and muscles, and preventing nutrient deficiencies.

Disease Prevention:
A nutritious diet is a cornerstone of disease prevention. By choosing nutrient-dense foods and minimizing the intake of processed foods, added sugars, and unhealthy fats, individuals can reduce the risk of developing chronic conditions such as obesity, heart disease, type 2 diabetes, hypertension, and certain types of cancer.

Weight Management:
In the quest for achieving and sustaining a healthy weight, the cornerstone lies in cultivating nutritious dietary practices. This journey toward better weight management entails a strategic approach, where the emphasis is placed on embracing whole, minimally processed foods while exercising portion control. By conscientiously monitoring calorie intake, individuals can navigate the path to weight loss or maintenance with greater efficacy.

Central to this endeavor is the prioritization of nutrient-rich foods, which serve as the building blocks of a balanced diet. These wholesome offerings not only fuel the body with essential vitamins and minerals but also play a pivotal role in promoting feelings of satiety. In essence, healthy eating habits serve as the bedrock upon which successful weight management endeavors are built. By embracing a diet rich in whole foods, individuals can embark on a journey toward improved health and well-being, one nourishing meal at a time.

Energy and Vitality:
Proper nutrition fuels the body and provides the energy needed for daily activities, exercise, and optimal performance. By nourishing the body with nutrient-rich foods, individuals can experience increased energy levels, improved concentration, better mood, and enhanced overall vitality.

Gut Health:
The foods we eat play a significant role in maintaining a healthy gut microbiome, which is essential for digestion, nutrient absorption, immune function, and overall well-being. A diet high in fiber from fruits, vegetables, whole grains, and legumes supports a diverse and healthy gut microbiota, while fermented foods like yogurt, kefir, and sauerkraut provide beneficial probiotics.

Longevity:
Healthy eating habits are associated with longevity and a reduced risk of premature death. By prioritizing nutrient-rich foods and adopting a balanced diet, individuals can support their long-term health and increase their chances of living a longer, healthier life.

In summary, healthy eating and selecting the right foods are critical components of a healthy lifestyle. By making informed choices about the foods we consume and prioritizing nutrient-dense options, we can support overall health, prevent disease, maintain a healthy weight, boost energy levels, support gut health, and enhance longevity.

VEGGIE KITCHEN BASICS: ESSENTIAL INGREDIENTS

Let's consider the key principles of preparing vegetarian dishes:

Utilization of Plant-Based Ingredients:
The cornerstone of vegetarian cuisine lies in plant-based ingredients such as fruits, vegetables, grains, legumes, nuts, and seeds. They form the foundation for creating diverse and nourishing dishes.

Alternative Sources of Protein:
Instead of meat, vegetarian cuisine relies on alternative sources of protein such as tofu, soy products, beans, lentils, chickpeas, peas, nuts, and seeds.

Richness in Flavors and Textures:
Vegetarian cuisine is renowned for its diversity of flavors and textures, thanks to a wide array of plant-based ingredients. Crafting dishes with various vegetables, grains, legumes, and nuts allows for unique and intriguing combinations.

Balance and Nutritional Value:
It is essential to ensure balance and nutritional value in vegetarian dishes. Including a variety of ingredients rich in vitamins, minerals, and other essential nutrients promotes dishes that are beneficial for health.

Use of Spices and Seasonings:
Spices and seasonings play a crucial role in vegetarian cuisine, imparting aroma, taste, and character to dishes. They enhance the flavors of plant-based ingredients and contribute to unique culinary compositions.

Experimentation and Creativity:
Vegetarian cuisine offers boundless opportunities for experimentation and culinary exploration. Try new recipes, ingredient combinations, and cooking techniques to expand your culinary repertoire and enrich your diet.

FOODS TO EAT AND AVOID

Foods to eat:

- Fruits: such as apples, bananas, oranges, berries, etc.

- Vegetables: such as leafy greens, broccoli, carrots, tomatoes, etc.

- Legumes: such as lentils, chickpeas, black beans, kidney beans, etc.

- Whole grains: such as brown rice, quinoa, oats, barley, etc.

- Nuts and seeds: such as almonds, walnuts, chia seeds, flax seeds, etc.

- Dairy products (for lacto-ovo vegetarians): such as milk, cheese, etc.

- Eggs (for ovo-vegetarians and lacto-ovo vegetarians)

Foods to limit or avoid:

- Meat: such as beef, pork, chicken, turkey, etc.

- Seafood: such as fish, shrimp, crab, etc.

- Animal-based fats: such as lard, butter, etc.

- Refined carbohydrates: such as white bread, white rice, pasta, etc.

- Highly processed foods: such as sugary snacks, chips, etc.

AIR FRYER ESSENTIALS: BASICS & BEYOND

The Air Fryer emerges as an indispensable kitchen tool for those adhering to a vegetarian lifestyle. This device offers the ability to fry a variety of vegetables, fruits, grains, legumes, nuts, and seeds with little to no oil, presenting dishes that are less greasy and healthier. Let's delve deeper into how the Air Fryer integrates into vegetarian diets and aids in maintaining a healthy lifestyle.

Principle of Air Fryer Operation:

Understanding the fundamentals of how an Air Fryer operates is essential for harnessing its full potential in the kitchen. At its core, an Air Fryer utilizes rapid air technology to circulate hot air around the food, creating a crispy outer layer while retaining moisture within.

The process begins as the Air Fryer's heating element heats the air inside the cooking chamber, generating intense heat. Once the desired temperature is reached, a powerful fan circulates the hot air at high speed, evenly distributing it across the food.

As the hot air surrounds the ingredients, it triggers the Maillard reaction—a chemical reaction between amino acids and reducing sugars that results in browning and flavor development. This reaction is what gives foods their characteristic golden-brown crispiness and savory taste.

Unlike traditional deep frying methods that submerge food in oil, air frying requires only a minimal amount of oil, if any at all. Instead, the circulating hot air rapidly evaporates moisture from the food's surface, creating a crispy texture reminiscent of deep-fried favorites, without the excess oil and calories.

Moreover, the versatility of an Air Fryer extends beyond just frying. Many models come equipped with additional cooking functions such as baking, grilling, roasting, and even dehydrating. This multifunctionality allows for a wide range of culinary possibilities, from crispy snacks to succulent main courses and even desserts.

Advantages of Using an Air Fryer in a Vegetarian Diet:

In the pursuit of healthier cooking methods, the Air Fryer emerges as a champion, offering a guilt-free way to indulge in crispy, delicious dishes without the excess oil and calories. By utilizing minimal or no oil, this innovative device transforms traditional frying techniques, preserving the nutritional integrity of ingredients while satisfying the palate.

Versatility is the hallmark of the Air Fryer, accommodating a wide array of foods ranging from vegetables and fruits to grains and legumes. With its adaptability, culinary enthusiasts can explore endless possibilities for crafting wholesome vegetarian dishes that are as nutritious as they are flavorful.

In the realm of convenience, the Air Fryer reigns supreme, operating swiftly and efficiently to streamline meal preparation. Its user-friendly design and easy-to-clean components make it a practical addition to any kitchen, offering time-saving solutions for busy lifestyles.

But beyond its practicality lies the true magic of the Air Fryer: its ability to elevate vegetarian cuisine to new heights. From crispy vegetable chips to golden-brown French fries, from tantalizing fruit chips to succulent roasted vegetables, the Air Fryer unlocks a world of culinary creativity, allowing for the creation of an array of healthy and delicious snacks, side dishes, and main courses.

In essence, the Air Fryer transcends mere functionality to become an indispensable tool in the vegetarian kitchen. With its promise of healthier frying methods and unparalleled convenience, it empowers individuals to enjoy their favorite flavors while adhering to a wholesome lifestyle. Embrace the possibilities, and let the Air Fryer become your trusted ally in the quest for culinary excellence and well-being.

Here are some suggestions for preparing nutritious meals using an Air Fryer:

Cooking vegetables in an Air Fryer is effortless and can accommodate a diverse array of produce, ranging from delicate beans to hearty root vegetables. For optimal cooking results, particularly with firmer vegetables, it's advisable to soak them in cold water for 15-20 minutes and then gently pat them dry with a clean kitchen towel.

Exploring the emerging culinary trend of air roasting is highly recommended, especially when preparing your favorite winter dishes.

To achieve consistent browning, remember to turn your foods halfway through the cooking process. Just like you would on a grill or in a skillet, flipping your ingredients ensures even cooking.

While your Air Fryer is capable of baking your preferred recipes, it's essential to consult the appliance's manual before using new bakeware with the Air Fryer.

Adjust the cooking time according to your desired level of doneness, as Air Fryer recipes are adaptable and suitable for all models. If you feel that the food requires additional cooking, make necessary adjustments and extend the cooking time by a few minutes. It's not essential to strictly adhere to recipe times, as ingredient sizes and textures can vary.

The cooking duration varies depending on your specific Air Fryer model, food size, pre-preparation steps, and other factors. For shorter cooking periods, preheat the Air Fryer for approximately 3-4 minutes. Conversely, if you start with a cold cooking basket, consider extending the cooking time by an additional 3 minutes.

For easy cleanup and enhanced flavor, utilize a high-quality oil spray to lightly coat food and the cooking basket.

BREAKFAST RECIPES

VEGETABLE OMELETTE

Cooking Difficulty: 2/10	Cooking Time: 11 minutes	Servings: 2

INGREDIENTS

- 4 eggs
- 1 small red bell pepper, diced
- 1 small tomato, diced
- 1/4 cup chopped spinach
- salt and pepper to taste

DESCRIPTION

STEP 1
Beat the eggs in a bowl. Add the diced red bell pepper, tomato, spinach, salt, and pepper. Mix well.

STEP 2
Evenly distribute the egg and vegetable mixture into a greased or parchment-lined baking dish.

STEP 3
Place the dish in the air fryer and cook at 180 degrees C (356 degrees F) for 8-10 minutes, or until the omelette is golden and firm.

STEP 4
After cooking, slice the omelette into portions and serve warm.

NUTRITIONAL INFORMATION

120 Calories, 8g Fat, 5g Carbs, 10g Protein

NUTRITIOUS FRUIT OATMEAL

Cooking Difficulty: 2/10

Cooking Time: 22 minutes

Servings: 2

INGREDIENTS

- 1/2 cup rolled oats
- 1 cup almond milk (or any other plant-based milk)
- 1 large apple, diced
- 1/2 teaspoon ground cinnamon
- 1 tablespoon honey or maple syrup (optional)
- a few raisins or dried fruit pieces for garnish (optional)

DESCRIPTION

STEP 1
In a bowl, mix together the rolled oats, almond milk, diced apple, and ground cinnamon.

STEP 2
Evenly distribute the mixture into two baking dishes, greased with oil or lined with parchment paper. Place the dishes in the air fryer and cook at 180 degrees C (356 degrees F) for 15-20 minutes, or until the oatmeal thickens and becomes tender.

STEP 3
After cooking, drizzle the oatmeal with honey or maple syrup, if using, and garnish with raisins or dried fruit pieces.

NUTRITIONAL INFORMATION

240 Calories, 5g Fat, 40g Carbs, 7g Protein

POTATO VEGETABLE OMELETTE

Cooking Difficulty: 2/10	Cooking Time: 18 minutes	Servings: 2

NUTRITIONAL INFORMATION

Calories 308, Fat 9.2g, Carbs 8g, Protein 11.2g

INGREDIENTS

- 2 medium potatoes
- 1 small onion
- 1 medium tomato
- 1 green bell pepper
- 4 eggs
- salt and pepper to taste
- fresh herbs for garnish (optional)

DESCRIPTION

STEP 1

Prepare the potatoes by slicing them into thin rounds or cubes. Dice the onion, tomato, and bell pepper into small pieces. Preheat the air fryer to 180 degrees Celsius (356 degrees Fahrenheit).

STEP 2

In a large bowl, beat the eggs and add the chopped vegetables, salt, and pepper. Mix thoroughly.

STEP 3

Evenly distribute the egg and vegetable mixture into a greased or parchment-lined baking dish.

STEP 4

Place the dish in the air fryer and cook at 356 degrees Fahrenheit for 10-12 minutes, or until the omelette is golden and firm.

STEP 5

Once the omelette is cooked, slice it into portions, garnish with fresh herbs if desired, and serve immediately. Enjoy your healthy breakfast for two!

BANANA OAT PANCAKES

Cooking Difficulty: 2/10	Cooking Time: 10 minutes	Servings: 2

INGREDIENTS

- 2 ripe bananas
- 1 cup rolled oats
- 1/2 cup almond milk (or any other plant-based milk)
- 1 teaspoon baking powder
- 1/2 teaspoon ground cinnamon
- 1/2 teaspoon vanilla extract
- maple syrup and sliced bananas for serving (optional)

DESCRIPTION

STEP 1

In a blender, combine the ripe bananas, rolled oats, almond milk, baking powder, ground cinnamon, and vanilla extract. Blend until smooth.

STEP 2

Preheat your air fryer to 180°C (356°F). Pour the pancake batter onto the air fryer basket, forming small pancakes.

STEP 3

Cook the pancakes in the air fryer for 5-7 minutes, flipping halfway through, until they are golden brown and cooked through. Serve the pancakes warm with maple syrup and sliced bananas.

NUTRITIONAL INFORMATION

200 Calories, 3g Fat, 27g Carbs, 5g Protein

AIR FRYER VEGGIE BREAKFAST BURRITOS

Cooking Difficulty: 2/10	Cooking Time: 25 minutes	Servings: 2

INGREDIENTS

- 4 large eggs
- 1/4 cup diced bell peppers (any color)
- 1/4 cup diced onions
- 1/4 cup diced tomatoes
- 1/4 cup chopped spinach
- 1/4 cup shredded cheese
- 1/2 teaspoon garlic powder
- salt and pepper to taste
- 2 large flour tortillas
- cooking spray

NUTRITIONAL INFORMATION

Calories: 350; Fat: 15 g; Carbs: 40 g; Protein: 15g

STEP 1

Preheat the air fryer to 180 degrees Celsius (356 degrees Fahrenheit).

STEP 2

In a bowl, whisk together the eggs, diced bell peppers, onions, tomatoes, chopped spinach, shredded cheese, garlic powder, salt, and pepper.

STEP 3

Spray the Air Fryer basket with cooking spray to prevent sticking.

STEP 4

Pour the egg mixture into the air fryer basket, spreading it evenly. Cook for 8-10 minutes or until the eggs are set and lightly golden on top.

STEP 5

Remove the cooked egg mixture from the air fryer and set aside.

STEP 6

Place a flour tortilla on a flat surface and spoon half of the cooked egg mixture onto the center of the tortilla. Fold the sides of the tortilla over the filling, then roll it up tightly to form a burrito. Repeat with the remaining tortilla and egg mixture.

STEP 7

Place the burritos seam-side down in the air fryer basket and cook for an additional 2-3 minutes to crisp up the tortillas.

STEP 8

Serve the air fryer veggie breakfast burritos hot, optionally with salsa or avocado slices on the side.

VEGGIE BREAKFAST HASH

Cooking Difficulty: 2/10

Cooking Time: 25 minutes

Servings: 2

INGREDIENTS

- 2 medium potatoes, diced
- 1 bell pepper, diced
- 1 onion, diced
- 1 cup diced mushrooms
- 2 cloves garlic, minced
- 2 tablespoons olive oil
- 1 teaspoon paprika
- salt and pepper to taste
- chopped parsley for garnish (optional)

DESCRIPTION

STEP 1
In a bowl, toss together the diced potatoes, bell pepper, onion, mushrooms, minced garlic, olive oil, paprika, salt, and pepper until evenly coated.

STEP 2
Preheat your air fryer to 200°C (390°F). Spread the vegetable mixture in a single layer in the air fryer basket. Cook for 15-20 minutes, shaking the basket halfway through, until the vegetables are golden brown and crispy.

STEP 3
Serve the veggie breakfast hash hot.

NUTRITIONAL INFORMATION

180 Calories, 7g Fat, 25g Carbs, 4g Protein

AVOCADO EGG BOATS

Cooking Difficulty: 2/10	Cooking Time: 8 minutes	Servings: 4

INGREDIENTS

- 4 avocado
- 4 eggs
- chopped chives
- chopped parsley
- pepper
- salt
- chopped parsley for garnish (optional)

DESCRIPTION

STEP 1
Warm up the fryer to 350°F.

STEP 2
Remove the pit from the avocado. Slice and scoop out part of the flesh. Shake with the seasonings.

STEP 3
Add an egg to each half and place in the preheated air fryer for 6 minutes.

STEP 4
Remove and serve with some additional parsley and chives if desired.

NUTRITIONAL INFORMATION

288 Calories, 26.4g Fat, 7.5g Carbs, 7g Protein

BLUEBERRY BREAKFAST MUFFINS

Cooking Difficulty: 2/10	Cooking Time: 15 minutes	Servings: 4

NUTRITIONAL INFORMATION

Calories 120, Fat 1g, Carbs 26g, Protein 3.2g

INGREDIENTS

- 1 cup whole wheat flour
- 1/2 cup rolled oats
- 1/4 cup honey or maple syrup
- 1 teaspoon baking powder
- 1/2 teaspoon baking soda
- 1/4 teaspoon salt
- 1/2 cup unsweetened applesauce
- 1/4 cup almond milk (or any other plant-based milk)
- 1 teaspoon vanilla extract
- 1 cup fresh blueberries

DESCRIPTION

STEP 1
Preheat your air fryer to 180°C (356°F). In a large mixing bowl, combine the whole wheat flour, rolled oats, baking powder, baking soda, and salt.

STEP 2
In a separate bowl, whisk together the honey or maple syrup, unsweetened applesauce, almond milk, and vanilla extract.

STEP 3
Pour the wet ingredients into the dry ingredients and mix until just combined.

STEP 4
Gently fold in the fresh blueberries. Divide the batter evenly among muffin cups lined with parchment paper liners.

STEP 5
Place the muffin tray in the air fryer and cook for 10-12 minutes, or until a toothpick inserted into the center of a muffin comes out clean. Allow the muffins to cool slightly before serving.

AVOCADO & TOMATO TOASTS

Cooking Difficulty: 1/10	Cooking Time: 10 minutes	Servings: 4

INGREDIENTS

- 4 slices of whole wheat bread
- 2 ripe avocados
- 2 tomatoes, sliced
- 1 lemon (juice)
- fresh basil for garnish
- salt and pepper to taste
- chopped parsley for garnish (optional)

DESCRIPTION

STEP 1
Spread a thin layer of avocado flesh on each slice of bread.

STEP 2
Place the bread in the air fryer basket, ensuring they do not overlap.

STEP 3
Top with slices of tomatoes. Drizzle with lemon juice. Start the air fryer for 5-7 minutes until the toast turns golden.

NUTRITIONAL INFORMATION

169 Calories, 2.5g Fat, 4.4g Carbs, 3.1g Protein

BERRY NUT OAT BALLS

Cooking Difficulty: 2/10	Cooking Time: 15 minutes	Servings: 8

INGREDIENTS

- 1 cup steel-cut oats
- 1/2 cup plant-based milk (oat or almond)
- 1 ripe banana, mashed
- 1/2 cup mixed berries (strawberries, raspberries, blueberries)
- 1/4 cup chopped nuts (walnuts, almonds)
- 1 tablespoon honey

DESCRIPTION

STEP 1
In a bowl, combine steel-cut oats, plant-based milk, and mashed banana. Add in the mixed berries and chopped nuts. Mix well.

STEP 2
Shape the mixture into small balls and place them in the air fryer basket. Start the air fryer for 10-12 minutes at 160°C.

STEP 3
Take out the oat balls from the air fryer. Drizzle each ball with honey or maple syrup.

NUTRITIONAL INFORMATION

340 Calories, 8.9g Fat, 6.2g Carbs, 11g Protein

VEGAN VEGGIE AND CHEESE BREAKFAST SANDWICH

Cooking Difficulty: 2/10	Cooking Time: 10 minutes	Servings: 2

NUTRITIONAL INFORMATION

Calories 300, Fat 10g, Carbs 27g, Protein 9g

INGREDIENTS

- 4 slices of whole grain bread
- 1 large tomato, sliced
- 1 small cucumber, thinly sliced
- 1 carrot, thinly sliced
- 1 red onion, sliced into rings
- 4 slices of vegan cheese
- 1 tablespoon olive oil
- salt and pepper to taste
- fresh herbs (dill, parsley) for garnish

DESCRIPTION

STEP 1
Preheat your air fryer to 180°C (356°F).

STEP 2
Place tomato, cucumber, carrot, and red onion slices on each slice of bread.

STEP 3
Add a slice of vegan cheese to each sandwich.

STEP 4
Drizzle with olive oil and season with salt and pepper to taste. Top each sandwich with the remaining slices of bread.

STEP 5
Place the sandwiches in the air fryer and cook for 5-7 minutes, until the bread is golden and crispy.

STEP 6
Serve hot sandwiches garnished with fresh herbs.

TOFU BREAKFAST

Cooking Difficulty: 2/10	Cooking Time: 27 minutes	Servings: 2

INGREDIENTS

- 200g tofu, diced
- 1 tablespoon soy sauce
- 1 teaspoon turmeric
- 1/2 teaspoon garlic powder
- 1/2 teaspoon paprika
- fresh herbs (cilantro, basil) for garnish
- slices of whole grain bread for serving

DESCRIPTION

STEP 1
In a bowl, mix together soy sauce, turmeric, garlic powder, and paprika. Toss the diced tofu in this mixture until well coated.

STEP 2
Preheat the air fryer to 200°C (392°F). Arrange the tofu cubes in a single layer on the bottom of the air fryer basket. Air fry the tofu for 15-20 minutes, flipping occasionally, until golden and crispy.

STEP 3
Serve the air-fried tofu hot, garnished with fresh herbs, and accompanied by slices of whole grain bread.

NUTRITIONAL INFORMATION

150 Calories, 10g Fat, 5g Carbs, 15g Protein

BREAKFAST SCRAMBLE

Cooking Difficulty: 2/10	Cooking Time: 23 minutes	Servings: 2

INGREDIENTS

- 200g firm tofu, crumbled
- 1 tablespoon olive oil
- 1 small red bell pepper, sliced
- 1 small green bell pepper, sliced
- 1 small carrot, thinly sliced
- 2 green onions, sliced
- 2 cloves garlic, minced
- 1 teaspoon turmeric
- 1/2 teaspoon cumin
- salt and pepper to taste
- fresh parsley for garnish

DESCRIPTION

STEP 1
Preheat the air fryer to 180°C (356°F).

STEP 2
In a bowl, mix the crumbled tofu with olive oil, red and green bell peppers, carrot, green onions, and garlic. Sprinkle with turmeric, cumin, salt, and pepper, and toss well to coat. Transfer the mixture to the air fryer and cook for 15-20 minutes, stirring occasionally, until the vegetables are tender and the tofu is golden.

STEP 3
Serve the hot breakfast scramble garnished with fresh parsley.

NUTRITIONAL INFORMATION

200 Calories, 8g Fat, 10g Carbs, 15g Protein

FRUIT OATMEAL BREAKFAST

Cooking Difficulty: 2/10

Cooking Time: 27 minutes

Servings: 2

INGREDIENTS

- 1 cup steel-cut oats
- 2 cups almond milk (or any other plant-based milk)
- 2 tablespoons maple syrup
- 1 teaspoon cinnamon
- 1/2 teaspoon vanilla extract
- 1 large pear, diced
- 1/4 cup dried apricots (or raisins)
- 1/4 cup chopped almonds (for garnish)

DESCRIPTION

STEP 1
In a large bowl, combine the steel-cut oats, almond milk, maple syrup, cinnamon, and vanilla extract.

STEP 2
Add the diced pear and dried apricots, and mix well. Transfer the mixture to the air fryer and cook for 20-25 minutes at 160°C (320°F), stirring occasionally, until the oatmeal becomes thick and creamy.

STEP 3
Serve the hot fruit oatmeal breakfast, garnished with chopped almonds.

NUTRITIONAL INFORMATION

275 Calories, 10g Fat, 40g Carbs, 7g Protein

AIR FRYER HASH BROWNS

Cooking Difficulty: 2/10	Cooking Time: 23 minutes	Servings: 2

INGREDIENTS

- 2 large potatoes, peeled and diced
- 1 onion, sliced
- 2 tablespoons olive oil
- 1/2 teaspoon garlic powder
- salt and pepper to taste

DESCRIPTION

STEP 1
Preheat your air fryer to 200°C (390°F).

STEP 2
In a large bowl, mix diced potatoes, sliced onion, olive oil, garlic powder, salt, and pepper. Transfer the mixture to the air fryer basket and cook for 15-20 minutes, stirring occasionally, until the hash browns are golden and crispy.

STEP 3
Serve the hot hash browns as a side dish or enjoy them on their own.

NUTRITIONAL INFORMATION

180 Calories, 6g Fat, 20g Carbs, 2g Protein

MAIN DISH

GRILLED EGGPLANT

Cooking Difficulty: 3/10	Cooking Time: 10 minutes	Servings: 4

INGREDIENTS

- 3 eggplant, sliced
- 2 tbsp. olive oil
- salt and pepper
- cherry tomatoes
- 1 tbsp. mint, chopped
- 1 tsp. red wine vinegar
- fresh parsley for garnish

DESCRIPTION

STEP 1

Coat the eggplant with oil and season with salt and pepper.

STEP 2

Air fry at 400°F for 10-15 minutes or until browned and cooked through.

STEP 3

Top the grilled eggplant with the minty salsa. Serve straight away.

NUTRITIONAL INFORMATION

Calories 71, Fat 5 g, Carbs 6 g, Protein 2 g

VEGGIE TOSTADAS WITH GUACAMOLE

Cooking Difficulty: 2/10	Cooking Time: 15 minutes	Servings: 2

NUTRITIONAL INFORMATION

Calories 300, Fat 10g, Carbs 27g, Protein 9g

INGREDIENTS

- 2 tortillas (wheat or corn)
- 1/2 red bell pepper, sliced into half rings
- 1/2 green bell pepper, sliced into half rings
- 1/2 red onion, sliced
- 1/2 teaspoon cumin
- 1/2 teaspoon chili powder
- salt and pepper to taste
- 1 tablespoon olive oil
- 1 large tomato, diced
- 1 avocado
- 1/2 lime, juice
- 1 clove garlic, minced
- fresh cilantro or parsley for serving
- 1/2 can of canned beans (e.g., black or red beans), rinsed and drained

DESCRIPTION

STEP 1
Preheat the air fryer to 200°C (390°F). In a large bowl, mix the red bell pepper, green bell pepper, red onion, cumin, chili powder, salt, pepper, and olive oil.

STEP 2
Spread the vegetable mixture evenly on the tortillas and carefully transfer them to the air fryer.

STEP 3
Cook the tostadas for 8-10 minutes or until the vegetables are tender and golden brown.

STEP 4
While the tostadas are cooking, prepare the guacamole. In a bowl, mash the avocado, add lime juice, minced garlic, salt, and pepper to taste. Mix well until smooth.

STEP 5
Once the tostadas are ready, top each one with diced tomatoes, beans, and a generous amount of guacamole. Serve the hot veggie tostadas with lime wedges.

BRUSSELS SPROUTS

Cooking Difficulty: 2/10	Cooking Time: 18 minutes	Servings: 2

INGREDIENTS

- 1 lb brussels sprouts, trimmed and halved
- 2 tablespoons olive oil
- 2 cloves garlic, minced
- 1/4 cup grated parmesan cheese
- salt and pepper to taste

DESCRIPTION

STEP 1

Preheat your air fryer to 200°C (390°F). In a large bowl, toss the Brussels sprouts with olive oil, minced garlic, grated Parmesan cheese, salt, and pepper until well coated. Place the seasoned Brussels sprouts in the air fryer basket in a single layer. Cook the Brussels sprouts in the air fryer for 12-15 minutes, shaking the basket halfway through cooking, until they are crispy and caramelized.

STEP 2

Once cooked, remove the Brussels sprouts from the air fryer and transfer them to a serving dish. Garnish with additional grated Parmesan cheese if desired

NUTRITIONAL INFORMATION

120 Calories, 8g Fat, 9g Carbs, 5g Protein

BBQ GRILLED CORN

 Cooking Difficulty: 1/10

 Cooking Time: 17 minutes

 Servings: 3

INGREDIENTS

- 6 ears of corn, peeled
- 1 tbsp olive oil
- 1 tsp garlic powder
- 1/4 cup BBQ sauce
- salt and pepper to taste
- cooking spray
- vegan cheese

DESCRIPTION

STEP 1
Preheat a deep fryer to 375°F. In a small bowl, mix olive oil and spices. Using a brush, spread the oil mixture over the corn cobs. Spray a deep fryer basket with cooking spray and place the corn in it.

STEP 2
Cook the corn in the deep fryer for 8 minutes. After that, brush the corn cobs with BBQ sauce and cook for another 4-6 minutes, until nicely crusted.

STEP 3
When the corn is ready, remove it from the fryer and transfer it to a serving platter. Serve on top garnished with vegan cheese.

NUTRITIONAL INFORMATION

180 Calories, 4g Fat, 2.5g Carbs, 3g Protein

VEGGIE QUESADILLAS

Cooking Difficulty: 2/10	Cooking Time: 11 minutes	Servings: 2

INGREDIENTS

- 4 small flour tortillas
- 1 cup shredded cheese (use vegan cheese for a vegan option)
- 1/2 cup black beans, drained and rinsed
- 1/2 cup corn kernels
- 1/2 cup diced bell peppers (any color)
- 1/4 cup diced red onion
- 1 teaspoon ground cumin
- 1 teaspoon chili powder
- salt and pepper to taste
- cooking spray or olive oil spray

NUTRITIONAL INFORMATION

Calories: 280; Fat: 15 g; Carbs: 32 g; Protein: 12g

STEP 1

In a mixing bowl, combine black beans, corn, bell peppers, red onion, ground cumin, chili powder, salt, and pepper. Mix well to combine.

STEP 2

Preheat your air fryer to 180°C (350°F).

STEP 3

Place two tortillas on a clean work surface. Sprinkle a layer of shredded cheese on each tortilla.

STEP 4

Spoon the vegetable and bean mixture evenly over the cheese layer on both tortillas.

STEP 5

Top each tortilla with another tortilla to form a quesadilla. Lightly coat both sides of each quesadilla with cooking spray or olive oil spray.

STEP 6

Carefully transfer the quesadillas to the air fryer basket. You may need to cook them in batches depending on the size of your air fryer.

STEP 7

Cook the quesadillas in the air fryer for 5-6 minutes, flipping halfway through, or until they are golden brown and crispy.

STEP 8

Once cooked, remove the quesadillas from the air fryer and let them cool slightly before slicing into wedges. Serve.

TOFU WITH VEGETABLES

Cooking Difficulty: 2/10	Cooking Time: 24 minutes	Servings: 2

INGREDIENTS

- 250g firm tofu, cubed
- 1 red bell pepper, sliced into strips
- 1 small zucchini, sliced into rounds
- 1 carrot, thinly sliced
- 1 red onion, sliced into half-moons
- 1/2 broccoli, separated into large florets
- 1 tablespoon olive oil
- salt and pepper to taste
- 1/2 teaspoon turmeric
- fresh basil for garnish

DESCRIPTION

STEP 1
Preheat the air fryer to 200°C (400°F). In a large bowl, combine the tofu cubes, red bell pepper strips, zucchini rounds, carrot slices, red onion half-moons, and broccoli florets. Drizzle with olive oil and toss to coat all the ingredients evenly. Season with salt, pepper, and turmeric, then toss again to distribute the seasoning.

STEP 2
Arrange the vegetable and tofu mixture evenly on the bottom of the air fryer basket.Air fry for 15-20 minutes or until cooked through, stirring occasionally to ensure even cooking. Once done, remove from the air fryer, sprinkle with fresh basil, and serve immediately.

NUTRITIONAL INFORMATION

180 Calories, 10g Fat, 12.5g Carbs, 12g Protein

COUSCOUS WITH VEGETABLES

Cooking Difficulty: 2/10	Cooking Time: 23 minutes	Servings: 2

INGREDIENTS

- 1 cup couscous
- 1.5 cups vegetable broth
- 1 red bell pepper, diced
- 1 large carrot, sliced into rounds
- 1 small zucchini, diced
- 1/2 red onion, thinly sliced
- 2 tablespoons olive oil
- 1 teaspoon salt
- 1/2 teaspoon black pepper
- 1/2 teaspoon turmeric
- fresh parsley for garnish

DESCRIPTION

STEP 1

In a large bowl, mix the couscous and vegetable broth. Let it sit for 5-10 minutes until the couscous absorbs all the broth. Add the diced red bell pepper, carrot rounds, diced zucchini, and thinly sliced red onion to the couscous. Drizzle with olive oil and season with salt, pepper, and turmeric. Mix well.

STEP 2

Transfer the couscous and vegetable mixture to the air fryer basket. Air fry in the air fryer at 180°C (360°F) for 15-20 minutes or until the vegetables are tender and the couscous is cooked. Garnish with fresh parsley before serving.

NUTRITIONAL INFORMATION

220 Calories, 7g Fat, 35g Carbs, 5g Protein

STUFFED SWEET POTATOES

Cooking Difficulty: 2/10	Cooking Time: 57 minutes	Servings: 2

INGREDIENTS

- 2 large sweet potatoes
- 1 tablespoon olive oil
- 1/2 cup sliced mushrooms
- 1/4 cup diced red bell pepper
- 1/4 cup diced red onion
- 1 clove garlic, minced
- 1/2 cup chickpea flour (or any other flour of your choice)
- salt and pepper to taste
- additional fillings of your choice: sliced tomatoes, corn, lentils, sliced olives, etc.
- toppings for serving: thick greek yogurt, sliced green onions, fresh herbs, and lemon wedges

NUTRITIONAL INFORMATION

Calories: 240; Fat: 5 g; Carbs: 75 g; Protein: 7g

DESCRIPTION

STEP 1
Preheat your air fryer to 200°C (390°F).

STEP 2
Wash the sweet potatoes and pierce them all over with a fork. Then wrap them in foil.

STEP 3
Place the sweet potatoes in the air fryer and bake them for 40-45 minutes, or until they are tender.

STEP 4
While the sweet potatoes are cooking, prepare the filling. Heat olive oil in a skillet and sauté mushrooms, red bell pepper, red onion, and garlic until softened. Season with salt and pepper to taste.

STEP 5
Add chickpea flour to the vegetables and cook for an additional 2-3 minutes until the filling thickens.

STEP 6
Remove the sweet potatoes from the air fryer and carefully slice them open lengthwise, but do not cut all the way through.

STEP 7
Begin stuffing the sweet potatoes with the prepared filling, then add additional toppings of your choice.

STEP 8
Serve the stuffed sweet potatoes with thick Greek yogurt, sliced green onions, fresh herbs, and lemon wedges.

BAKED VEGETABLES

Cooking Difficulty: 1/10	Cooking Time: 24 minutes	Servings: 2

INGREDIENTS

- 2 large potatoes
- 1 large carrot
- 1 small red onion
- 1 large tomato
- 2 tablespoons olive oil
- 2 teaspoons dried herbs (thyme, rosemary, basil)
- salt and pepper to taste

DESCRIPTION

STEP 1
Preheat the air fryer to 200°C (400°F).

STEP 2
Cut the potatoes and carrot into chunks, and the red onion into semi-circles. Cut the tomato into wedges. In a large bowl, toss the chopped vegetables with olive oil and dried herbs. Season with salt and pepper to taste, and mix well.

STEP 3
Arrange the vegetables evenly in the air fryer basket. Bake for 20-25 minutes or until the vegetables are golden and tender. Garnish with fresh herbs before serving, if desired.

NUTRITIONAL INFORMATION

180 Calories, 7g Fat, 25.5g Carbs, 3g Protein

BAKED SWEET POTATOES WITH MASHED AVOCADO

Cooking Difficulty: 2/10	Cooking Time: 10 minutes	Servings: 4

NUTRITIONAL INFORMATION

Calories 300, Fat 10g, Carbs 27g, Protein 9g

INGREDIENTS

- 4 large sweet potatoes
- 2 tablespoons olive oil
- salt and pepper to taste
- 2 avocados, peeled and mashed
- juice of 1 lemon
- 1/2 teaspoon chili powder (or to taste)

DESCRIPTION

STEP 1
Preheat your air fryer to 200°C (400°F). Wash the sweet potatoes and pierce them all over with a fork. Place them on a baking sheet, drizzle with olive oil, and season with salt and pepper to taste.

STEP 2
Air fry the sweet potatoes for 45-50 minutes, or until they are soft and golden.

STEP 3
While the sweet potatoes are cooking, prepare the mashed avocado. In a bowl, combine mashed avocados with lemon juice and chili powder. Mix well to combine.

STEP 4
Once the sweet potatoes are done, remove them from the air fryer and let them cool slightly. Then, slice each sweet potato lengthwise down the middle, without cutting all the way through.

STEP 5
Fill each sweet potato with the mashed avocado mixture. Enjoy!

QUINOA STUFFED BELL PEPPERS

Cooking Difficulty: 2/10	Cooking Time: 24 minutes	Servings: 4

INGREDIENTS

- 4 large bell peppers, halved and seeds removed
- 1 cup quinoa, cooked
- 1 can (15 oz) black beans, drained and rinsed
- 1 cup corn kernels (fresh or frozen)
- 1 cup cherry tomatoes, halved
- 1/2 cup red onion, finely chopped
- 1/2 cup fresh cilantro, chopped
- 1 teaspoon cumin
- salt and pepper to taste
- 1 cup tomato sauce (for topping)

DESCRIPTION

STEP 1
In a large mixing bowl, combine cooked quinoa, black beans, corn, cherry tomatoes, red onion, cilantro, cumin, salt, and pepper. Mix well. Stuff each bell pepper half with the quinoa mixture.

STEP 2
Preheat the air fryer at 180°C. Place the stuffed bell peppers in the air fryer basket. Cook for 15-20 minutes until the peppers are tender.

NUTRITIONAL INFORMATION

Calories 295, Fat 8 g, Carbs 11 g, Protein 9 g

ROASTED SWEET POTATOES AND BROCCOLI

Cooking Difficulty: 2/10	Cooking Time: 25 minutes	Servings: 2

INGREDIENTS

- 2 medium sweet potatoes, diced
- 1 head of broccoli, separated into small florets
- 2 tablespoons olive oil
- 1 teaspoon spice mix (smoked paprika, garlic powder, salt, pepper)

DESCRIPTION

STEP 1

Preheat the air fryer to 200°C (392°F). In a large bowl, toss diced sweet potatoes, broccoli florets, olive oil, and the spice mix. Ensure an even coating of oil and spices on the ingredients.

STEP 2

Place the sweet potatoes and broccoli in the air fryer basket, allowing space for air circulation.Start the air fryer for 20 minutes; the cooking time may vary based on the device's power. Stir periodically for even roasting.

NUTRITIONAL INFORMATION

Calories: 90; Fat: 3.3 g; Carbs: 9.1 g; Protein: 3.6 g

CRISPY TOFU WITH SOY-GINGER GLAZE

Cooking Difficulty: 3/10	Cooking Time: 28 minutes	Servings: 2

NUTRITIONAL INFORMATION

Calories 220, Fat 12g, Carbs 14g, Protein 16g

INGREDIENTS

- 1 block firm tofu, drained and cubed
- 2 cloves garlic, minced
- 2 tablespoons soy sauce
- 1 tablespoon sesame oil
- 1 tablespoon rice vinegar
- 1 tablespoon honey or maple syrup (optional)
- 1 tablespoon cornstarch
- 2 tablespoons water
- sesame seeds and sliced green onions, for garnish (optional)

DESCRIPTION

STEP 1
Preheat air fryer to 200°C (390°F).

STEP 2
Place tofu cubes in air fryer basket and cook for 15-20 minutes until crispy.

STEP 3
While tofu cooks, sauté minced garlic in a saucepan.

STEP 4
Add soy sauce, sesame oil, rice vinegar, and honey to the saucepan. Simmer for 2-3 minutes.

STEP 5
Mix cornstarch and water, then add to the sauce. Cook until thickened.

STEP 6
Once tofu is crispy, transfer to a plate.

STEP 7
Drizzle with soy-ginger glaze.

BAKED POTATO

Cooking Difficulty: 1/10	Cooking Time: 19 minutes	Servings: 2

INGREDIENTS

- 2-3 medium-sized potatoes
- 1-2 tablespoons olive oil
- Salt and pepper to taste
- Optional seasonings: garlic powder, paprika, or any other herbs and spices you prefer

DESCRIPTION

STEP 1
Start by preheating the fryer to 400°F. Wash the potatoes thoroughly and cut them in half and then cut each half into 3 pieces.

STEP 2
Mix the olive oil with the salt and the rest of the spices of your choice, add the potatoes, and mix thoroughly. Arrange the potato slices in the basket of the deep fryer in a single layer. Cook for 10-15 minutes, turning it halfway through the cooking time.

STEP 3
After cooking, transfer the potato slices to a plate lined with a paper towel to soak up the excess oil. Allow them to cool slightly before serving.

NUTRITIONAL INFORMATION

Calories: 147, Fat: 3.7g, Carbs: 26.7g, Protein: 3g

CRISPY TOFU STIR-FRY

Cooking Difficulty: 3/10	Cooking Time: 32 minutes	Servings: 4

INGREDIENTS

- 1 block firm tofu, pressed and cubed
- 1 cup broccoli florets
- 1 bell pepper
- 1 carrot
- 3 tablespoons soy sauce
- 1 tablespoon maple syrup
- 1 tablespoon rice vinegar
- 1 teaspoon sesame oil
- 1 teaspoon ginger, minced
- 1 cloves garlic, minced
- 1 tablespoons cornstarch
- sesame seeds and green onions for garnish
- cooked brown rice for serving

DESCRIPTION

STEP 1
In a bowl, toss tofu cubes with cornstarch until evenly coated. Place the tofu in the air fryer basket and air fry at 200°C for 15-20 minutes or until crispy, shaking the basket occasionally for even cooking.

STEP 2
In a separate bowl, mix soy sauce, maple syrup, rice vinegar, sesame oil, ginger, and garlic to create the stir-fry sauce. In the last 5 minutes of tofu cooking, add broccoli, bell pepper, and carrot to the air fryer, tossing in the sauce.

STEP 3
Continue air frying until the vegetables are tender-crisp.

NUTRITIONAL INFORMATION

Calories 295, Fat 8 g, Carbs 11 g, Protein 9 g

MUSHROOM AND SPINACH QUESADILLAS

Cooking Difficulty: 3/10	Cooking Time: 20 minutes	Servings: 2

INGREDIENTS

- 4 large flour tortillas
- 1 cup sliced mushrooms
- 2 cups fresh spinach leaves
- 1 cup shredded cheese (cheddar, mozzarella, or your choice)
- 1/2 red onion, thinly sliced
- 1 clove garlic, minced
- 1 tablespoon olive oil
- salt and pepper to taste
- salsa, guacamole, or sour cream for serving (optional)

NUTRITIONAL INFORMATION

Calories: 380; Fat: 19 g; Carbs: 38 g; Protein: 16g

STEP 1

Heat olive oil in a large skillet over medium heat. Add the sliced mushrooms and cook for 5-7 minutes, until they are tender and golden brown. Stir in the minced garlic and cook for an additional 1-2 minutes.

STEP 2

Add the fresh spinach leaves to the skillet and cook until wilted, about 2-3 minutes. Season with salt and pepper to taste. Remove from heat and set aside.

STEP 3

Place one flour tortilla on a flat surface. Sprinkle shredded cheese evenly over half of the tortilla. Top with a layer of the mushroom and spinach mixture, followed by a few slices of red onion. Fold the tortilla in half to cover the filling.

STEP 4

Repeat the process with the remaining tortillas and filling ingredients.

STEP 5

Preheat the air fryer to 180°C (360°F). Carefully transfer the assembled quesadillas to the air fryer basket, making sure they are not overlapping.

STEP 6

Air fry the quesadillas for 5-7 minutes, or until the tortillas are crispy and golden brown, and the cheese is melted.

STEP 7

Remove the quesadillas from the air fryer and let them cool for a minute before slicing into wedges. Serve the mushroom and spinach quesadillas hot, with salsa, guacamole, or sour cream on the side if desired.

RAINBOW BELL PEPPER STRIPS

Cooking Difficulty: 1/10	Cooking Time: 19 minutes	Servings: 2

INGREDIENTS

- 2 large bell peppers (one of each color), cleaned and sliced into strips
- 1 tablespoon olive oil
- 1 teaspoon salt
- 1 teaspoon black pepper

DESCRIPTION

STEP 1
Preheat the air fryer to 200°C (390°F). In a large bowl, toss the sliced bell peppers with olive oil, salt, and black pepper until evenly coated.

STEP 2
Arrange the bell pepper strips in a single layer in the air fryer basket.
Air fry the bell pepper strips for 15-20 minutes, shaking the basket occasionally, until the peppers are tender and the edges begin to brown.

STEP 3
Once cooked, transfer the peppers to a plate and serve as a side dish or garnish.

NUTRITIONAL INFORMATION

Calories: 70, Fat: 4g, Carbs: 7g, Protein: 1g

VEGETABLE PATTIES

Cooking Difficulty: 3/10	Cooking Time: 19 minutes	Servings: 2

INGREDIENTS

- 1 large carrot, grated
- 1 medium potato, grated
- 1/2 red onion, finely chopped
- 1 clove garlic, minced
- 1/4 cup breadcrumbs
- 1/4 cup vegan mayonnaise
- 1 tablespoon vegetable oil
- salt and pepper to taste

DESCRIPTION

STEP 1
In a large bowl, combine the grated carrot, potato, red onion, garlic, breadcrumbs, vegan mayonnaise, and seasonings. Form the mixture into small patties.

STEP 2
Preheat the air fryer to 180°C (360°F). Arrange the patties evenly in the air fryer basket. Air fry the patties for 12-15 minutes, flipping them halfway through, until they are evenly browned and cooked through.

STEP 3
Serve hot with your favorite sauce or dip.

NUTRITIONAL INFORMATION

180 Calories, 8g Fat, 25g Carbs, 3g Protein

ZUCCHINI FRITTERS

Cooking Difficulty: 2/10	Cooking Time: 16 minutes	Servings: 2

INGREDIENTS

- 1 medium zucchini, grated
- 1 carrot, grated
- 1 small onion, finely chopped
- 2 cloves garlic, minced
- 2 eggs
- 1/4 cup grated cheese (such as parmesan or cheddar)
- 3 tablespoons all-purpose flour
- 1/2 teaspoon salt
- 1/4 teaspoon pepper
- vegetable oil for greasing

DESCRIPTION

STEP 1
Squeeze excess moisture from the grated zucchini using a fine mesh sieve. In a large bowl, combine the zucchini, carrot, onion, garlic, eggs, cheese, flour, salt, and pepper until well combined.

STEP 2
Preheat the air fryer to 180°C (360°F). Grease the air fryer basket with vegetable oil. Spoon portions of the batter into the air fryer basket, spacing them apart for even cooking.

STEP 3
Air fry the fritters for about 10-12 minutes, flipping them halfway through cooking, until they are golden brown and crispy.

NUTRITIONAL INFORMATION

Calories: 120, Fat: 6g, Carbs: 4g, Protein: 6g

AIR FRYER FALAFEL

Cooking Difficulty: 3/10	Cooking Time: 20 minutes	Servings: 2

INGREDIENTS

- 1 can (15 oz) chickpeas, drained and rinsed
- 1/4 cup fresh parsley, chopped
- 1/4 cup fresh cilantro, chopped
- 2 cloves garlic, minced
- 1 small onion, chopped
- 1 teaspoon ground cumin
- 1 teaspoon ground coriander
- 1/2 teaspoon paprika
- 2 tablespoons chickpea flour or all-purpose flour
- salt and pepper to taste
- olive oil spray

NUTRITIONAL INFORMATION

Calories: 225; Fat: 5g; Carbs: 35g; Protein: 10g

DESCRIPTION

STEP 1

In a food processor, combine chickpeas, parsley, cilantro, garlic, onion, cumin, coriander, paprika, flour, salt, and pepper. Pulse until the mixture is well combined but still slightly chunky.

STEP 2

Using your hands, shape the mixture into small falafel balls.

STEP 3

Preheat your air fryer to 180°C (360°F).

STEP 4

Lightly spray the air fryer basket with olive oil spray.

STEP 5

Arrange the falafel balls in the air fryer basket in a single layer, leaving some space between each falafel.

STEP 6

Lightly spray the tops of the falafel balls with olive oil spray.

STEP 7

Air fry the falafel for 12-15 minutes, flipping halfway through cooking, until golden brown and crispy.

STEP 8

Once cooked, remove the falafel from the air fryer and serve hot with your favorite dipping sauce or in a pita with salad.

BRUSSELS SPROUTS WITH MUSHROOMS

Cooking Difficulty: 2/10	Cooking Time: 25 minutes	Servings: 2

INGREDIENTS

- 250g brussels sprouts, halved
- 200g mushrooms, halved
- 2 tbsp olive oil
- 2 cloves garlic, minced
- salt and pepper to taste
- fresh herbs (parsley, thyme, or rosemary), chopped
- juice of half a lemon

DESCRIPTION

STEP 1
Preheat your air fryer to 180°C (360°F). In a large bowl, toss Brussels sprouts, mushrooms, olive oil, and minced garlic until evenly coated.

STEP 2
Spread the vegetables evenly on the air fryer tray in a single layer. Season with salt and pepper. Air fry for 15-20 minutes until Brussels sprouts are golden and tender, and mushrooms are cooked through. Stir the vegetables occasionally for even cooking. Once done, sprinkle with fresh herbs and lemon juice before serving.

NUTRITIONAL INFORMATION

Calories 120, Fat 8g, Carbs 9g, Protein 4g

SWISS CHARD PATTIES

Cooking Difficulty: 2/10	Cooking Time: 18 minutes	Servings: 2

INGREDIENTS

- 200g swiss chard, chopped
- 1 onion, finely chopped
- 2 cloves garlic, minced
- 1 cup breadcrumbs or crushed crackers
- 2 eggs
- salt and pepper to taste
- oil for frying

DESCRIPTION

STEP 1
In a large bowl, mix together Swiss chard, onion, garlic, breadcrumbs or crushed crackers, eggs, salt, and pepper until well combined. Shape the mixture into patties.

STEP 2
Preheat your air fryer to 180°C (350°F). Lightly coat the air fryer basket with cooking spray. Place the patties in the air fryer basket in a single layer, ensuring they are not overcrowded.

STEP 3
Air fry the patties at 180°C (350°F) for 12-15 minutes, flipping halfway through, until they are golden brown and cooked through.Serve.

NUTRITIONAL INFORMATION

Calories: 150, Fat: 6g, Carbs: 8g, Protein: 6g

CRISPY TOFU NUGGETS

Cooking Difficulty: 3/10	Cooking Time: 25 minutes	Servings: 2

NUTRITIONAL INFORMATION

Calories 120, Fat 4g, Carbs 11g, Protein 9g

INGREDIENTS

- 1 block firm tofu, pressed and cut into cubes
- 1/4 cup cornstarch
- 1 tsp garlic powder
- 1 tsp paprika
- 1/2 tsp salt
- 1/4 tsp black pepper
- cooking spray

DESCRIPTION

STEP 1
Preheat the air fryer to 200°C (400°F).

STEP 2
In a shallow bowl, mix together the cornstarch, garlic powder, paprika, salt, and black pepper.

STEP 3
Roll each tofu cube in the cornstarch mixture until evenly coated.

STEP 4
Add soy sauce, sesame oil, rice Place the coated tofu cubes in a single layer in the air fryer basket, leaving space between each cube. Lightly spray the tofu cubes with cooking spray.

STEP 5
Air fry for 15-20 minutes, flipping halfway through, until the tofu is crispy and golden brown.

STEP 6
Once done, remove the tofu nuggets from the air fryer and let them cool slightly before serving. Serve the crispy tofu nuggets with your favorite dipping sauce and enjoy!

CARROT PATTIES

Cooking Difficulty: 3/10	Cooking Time: 17 minutes	Servings: 2

INGREDIENTS

- 2 medium carrots, peeled and sliced
- 1 onion, finely chopped
- 1 clove garlic, minced
- 1/2 cup finely chopped parsley
- 1/2 cup dry breadcrumbs
- 1 egg
- salt and pepper to taste
- 2 tablespoons olive oil

DESCRIPTION

STEP 1
Preheat the air fryer to 190°C (375°F). In a large bowl, combine the carrots, onion, garlic, parsley, breadcrumbs, and egg. Season the mixture with salt and pepper to taste and mix well.

STEP 2
Form the mixture into small patties. Grease the air fryer basket with olive oil. Arrange the patties evenly in the basket. Air fry the patties for about 10-12 minutes, flipping them halfway through, until they are golden brown and crispy.

STEP 3
Serve the carrot patties hot.

NUTRITIONAL INFORMATION

180 Calories, 10g Fat, 20g Carbs, 4g Protein

QUINOA VEGGIE PATTIES

Cooking Difficulty: 3/10	Cooking Time: 18 minutes	Servings: 2

INGREDIENTS

- 1 cup cooked quinoa
- 1 cup mixed vegetables (such as carrots, peas, corn), finely chopped
- 1/2 cup grated cheese (optional)
- 1/4 cup breadcrumbs
- 1 egg
- 2 cloves garlic, minced
- 2 tablespoons chopped fresh herbs (such as parsley, cilantro, or basil)
- salt and pepper to taste
- 2 tablespoons olive oil

DESCRIPTION

STEP 1
In a large bowl, combine the cooked quinoa, mixed vegetables, grated cheese, breadcrumbs, egg, minced garlic, and chopped fresh herbs. Season the mixture with salt and pepper to taste and mix well until everything is evenly combined. Form the mixture into small patties.

STEP 2
Preheat the air fryer to 190°C (375°F). Grease the air fryer basket with olive oil. Arrange the quinoa patties evenly in the basket. Air fry the patties for about 10-12 minutes, flipping them halfway through, until they are golden brown and crispy.

NUTRITIONAL INFORMATION

Calories: 280, Fat: 14g, Carbs: 28g, Protein: 12g

CHICKPEA AND VEGETABLE

Cooking Difficulty: 3/10	Cooking Time: 25 minutes	Servings: 2

INGREDIENTS

- 1 can (15 oz) chickpeas, drained and rinsed
- 1 tablespoon olive oil
- 1 teaspoon ground cumin
- 1/2 teaspoon paprika
- Salt and pepper, to taste
- 2 cups mixed salad greens
- 1 cucumber, diced
- 1 bell pepper, diced
- 1/4 cup cherry tomatoes, halved
- 1/4 cup red onion, thinly sliced
- 2 tablespoons fresh parsley, chopped
- 2 tablespoons lemon juice
- 1 tablespoon tahini
- 1 clove garlic, minced
- 1 tablespoon water

NUTRITIONAL INFORMATION

Calories: 320; Fat: 12g; Carbs: 38 g; Protein: 12g

STEP 1

Preheat the air fryer to 400°F (200°C).

STEP 2

In a mixing bowl, toss the chickpeas with olive oil, ground cumin, paprika, salt, and pepper until evenly coated.

STEP 3

Spread the seasoned chickpeas in a single layer in the air fryer basket.

STEP 4

Air fry the chickpeas for 15-20 minutes, shaking the basket halfway through, until they are crispy and golden brown.

STEP 5

In a large salad bowl, combine the mixed salad greens, diced cucumber, diced bell pepper, cherry tomatoes, red onion, and fresh parsley.

STEP 6

Pour the dressing over the salad ingredients and toss to coat evenly. Once the chickpeas are done, let them cool slightly before adding them to the salad.

STEP 7

Add the crispy chickpeas to the salad and gently toss to combine.

STEP 8

Serve the crispy chickpea and vegetable salad immediately, and enjoy a flavorful and nutritious meal!

AIR FRYER ASPARAGUS SPEARS

	Cooking Difficulty: 1/10		Cooking Time: 12 minutes		Servings: 2

INGREDIENTS

- 1 bunch of asparagus spears
- 1 tablespoon olive oil
- 2 cloves garlic, minced
- salt and pepper to taste
- lemon wedges (optional)

DESCRIPTION

STEP 1
Preheat the air fryer to 200°C (390°F). Wash the asparagus spears and trim off the tough ends. In a large bowl, toss the asparagus spears with olive oil, minced garlic, salt, and pepper until evenly coated.

STEP 2
Arrange the seasoned asparagus spears in a single layer in the air fryer basket. Air fry the asparagus for 7-10 minutes, shaking the basket halfway through the cooking time, until the spears are tender and slightly crispy. Remove the asparagus from the air fryer and transfer them to a serving platter.

NUTRITIONAL INFORMATION

70 Calories, 3g Fat, 9g Carbs, 4g Protein

CRISPY AIR FRYER PORTOBELLO MUSHROOMS

	Cooking Difficulty: 2/10		Cooking Time: 16 minutes		Servings: 2

NUTRITIONAL INFORMATION

Calories 65, Fat 4g, Carbs 7g, Protein 3g

INGREDIENTS

- 2 large portobello mushrooms
- 2 tablespoons olive oil
- 2 cloves garlic, minced
- 1 teaspoon dried thyme
- salt and pepper to taste
- fresh parsley, chopped (for garnish, optional)
- balsamic glaze (for serving, optional)

DESCRIPTION

STEP 1
Preheat the air fryer to 200°C (390°F).

STEP 2
Clean the portobello mushrooms and remove the stems. In a small bowl, whisk together the olive oil, minced garlic, dried thyme, salt, and pepper.

STEP 3
Brush the mushroom caps with the olive oil mixture, ensuring they are evenly coated on both sides.

STEP 4
Place the mushrooms in the air fryer basket, cap side down.

STEP 5
Air fry the mushrooms for 10-12 minutes, flipping halfway through the cooking time, until they are tender and crispy around the edges. Once done, remove the mushrooms from the air fryer and transfer them to a serving plate.

STEP 6
Garnish with fresh parsley and drizzle with balsamic glaze, if desired.

ERINGI MUSHROOMS

Cooking Difficulty: 2/10	Cooking Time: 15 minutes	Servings: 2

INGREDIENTS

- 200g eringi mushrooms, sliced
- 1 tablespoon olive oil
- 1 teaspoon garlic powder
- 1/2 teaspoon paprika
- salt and pepper to taste
- fresh parsley for garnish (optional)

DESCRIPTION

STEP 1

Preheat the air fryer to 200°C (390°F). In a bowl, toss the sliced eringi mushrooms with olive oil, garlic powder, paprika, salt, and pepper until evenly coated. Arrange the seasoned mushrooms in a single layer in the air fryer basket.

STEP 2

Air fry the mushrooms for 8-10 minutes, shaking the basket halfway through cooking, until they are golden brown and crispy. Once done, remove the mushrooms from the air fryer and transfer them to a serving plate. Garnish with fresh parsley if desired. Serve hot and enjoy!

NUTRITIONAL INFORMATION

Calories: 80, Fat: 6g, Carbs: 6g, Protein: 2g

AIR FRYER CORN COBS

Cooking Difficulty: 1/10	Cooking Time: 21 minutes	Servings: 2

INGREDIENTS

- 2 corn cobs
- 2 tablespoons olive oil
- salt and pepper to taste
- fresh herbs for garnish (optional)

DESCRIPTION

STEP 1

Preheat the air fryer to 200°C (390°F). Peel back the husks and remove the silk from the corn cobs. Cut each corn cob in half. Brush the corn with olive oil, ensuring an even coating.Season with salt and pepper to taste.

STEP 2

Place the corn halves in the air fryer basket, leaving space between them. Air fry the corn for 15-20 minutes, flipping halfway through, until golden brown. Once cooked, remove the corn from the air fryer and transfer to a plate. Garnish with fresh herbs, if desired.

NUTRITIONAL INFORMATION

120 Calories, 5g Fat, 20g Carbs, 3g Protein

SNACKS & DESSERTS

BEET CHIPS IN THE AIR FRYER

Cooking Difficulty: 2/10	Cooking Time: 25 minutes	Servings: 2

NUTRITIONAL INFORMATION

Calories 80, Fat 4g, Carbs 7g, Protein 1g

INGREDIENTS

- 2 medium beets
- 1 tablespoon olive oil
- salt and pepper to taste
- fresh herbs for garnish (optional)

DESCRIPTION

STEP 1
Preheat the air fryer to 180°C (350°F).

STEP 2
On a cutting board, slice the beets into thin slices about 1 millimeter thick.

STEP 3
In a large bowl, toss the sliced beets with olive oil until evenly coated. Season the beets with salt and pepper to taste.

STEP 4
Arrange the beet slices in a single layer in the air fryer basket, ensuring they are not overcrowded.

STEP 5
Air fry the beet chips for 15-20 minutes, flipping halfway through, until they are crispy and golden brown.

STEP 6
Once cooked, remove the beet chips from the air fryer and transfer them to a paper towel to remove any excess oil. Serve the hot beet chips, garnished with fresh herbs if desired.

SPICED AIR FRYER NUTS

Cooking Difficulty: 1/10	Cooking Time: 12 minutes	Servings: 2

INGREDIENTS

- 1 cup mixed nuts (such as almonds, cashews, and pecans)
- 1 tablespoon olive oil or melted coconut oil
- 1 teaspoon ground cinnamon
- 1/2 teaspoon ground cumin
- 1/4 teaspoon ground ginger
- 1/4 teaspoon cayenne pepper (adjust to taste)
- 1/2 teaspoon sea salt

DESCRIPTION

STEP 1

Preheat air fryer to 160°C (320°F). Toss nuts with oil until coated. Combine spices in a bowl. Sprinkle spice mix over nuts, toss to coat.

STEP 2

Coat air fryer basket with cooking spray. Spread nuts in a single layer in basket. Air fry for 8-10 minutes, shaking halfway. Watch carefully to prevent burning.Cool before serving.

NUTRITIONAL INFORMATION

Calories: 220, Fat: 19g, Carbs:g, Protein: 6g

SWEET POTATO CHIPS

Cooking Difficulty: 1/10	Cooking Time: 18 minutes	Servings: 2

INGREDIENTS

- 1 large sweet potato
- 1 tbsp olive oil or coconut oil
- 1/2 tsp brown sugar (optional)
- 1/2 tsp ground coriander
- 1/4 tsp turmeric
- salt and pepper to taste

DESCRIPTION

STEP 1

Preheat the air fryer to 190°C (375°F). Wash the sweet potato thoroughly and pat it dry. Slice the sweet potato into thin slices or rings. In a large bowl, mix the olive oil, brown sugar (if using), ground coriander, turmeric, salt, and pepper. Add the sliced sweet potato to the bowl and toss until evenly coated with the oil mixture.

STEP 2

Arrange the sweet potato in a single layer in the air fryer basket. Air fry the sweet potato for 12-15 minutes, flipping occasionally for even cooking.Carefully remove the cooked chips from the air fryer and let them cool slightly before serving.

NUTRITIONAL INFORMATION

120 Calories, 3g Fat, 22g Carbs, 2g Protein

POPCORN CAULIFLOWER

 Cooking Difficulty: 2/10

 Cooking Time: 25 minutes

 Servings: 2

NUTRITIONAL INFORMATION

Calories 180, Fat 4g, Carbs 22g, Protein 10g

INGREDIENTS

- 1 small head cauliflower
- 1/2 cup breadcrumbs
- 1/4 cup grated parmesan cheese
- 1 tsp garlic powder
- 1/2 tsp paprika
- salt and pepper to taste
- 2 eggs, beaten

DESCRIPTION

STEP 1
Preheat the air fryer to 200°C (400°F).

STEP 2
Cut the cauliflower into bite-sized florets.

STEP 3
In a bowl, mix the breadcrumbs, Parmesan cheese, garlic powder, paprika, salt, and pepper.

STEP 4
Dip each cauliflower floret into the beaten eggs, then coat it with the breadcrumb mixture.

STEP 5
Place the coated cauliflower florets in a single layer in the air fryer basket.

STEP 6
Air fry for 15-20 minutes, shaking the basket halfway through, until the cauliflower is crispy and golden brown. Serve hot and enjoy your delicious popcorn cauliflower!

APPLE CHIPS

Cooking Difficulty: 1/10	Cooking Time: 15 minutes	Servings: 2

INGREDIENTS

- 2 large apples
- 1 tsp cinnamon
- 1/2 tsp sugar (optional)

DESCRIPTION

STEP 1

Preheat air fryer to 160°C (320°F). Slice apples thinly and toss with cinnamon (and sugar if using).

STEP 2

Arrange slices in a single layer in air fryer basket. Air fry for 10-12 minutes, flipping halfway. Cool before serving.

NUTRITIONAL INFORMATION

Calories: 50, Fat: 0g, Carbs: 14g, Protein: 0g

VEGAN CHEESECAKE

Cooking Difficulty: 2/10	Cooking Time: 30 minutes	Servings: 2

NUTRITIONAL INFORMATION

Calories 460, Fat 36g, Carbs 29g, Protein 8g

INGREDIENTS

- 1 cup raw cashews, soaked overnight
- 1/4 cup coconut cream
- 1/4 cup maple syrup
- 2 tbsp lemon juice
- 1 tsp vanilla extract
- 1/4 cup coconut oil, melted
- 1/2 cup crushed graham crackers or digestive biscuits
- fresh fruit for topping (optional)

DESCRIPTION

STEP 1
Drain the soaked cashews and add them to a blender along with the coconut cream, maple syrup, lemon juice, and vanilla extract. Blend until smooth and creamy.

STEP 2
Line a small round cake pan or silicone mold with parchment paper and press the crushed graham crackers into the bottom to form the crust.Pour the cashew mixture over the crust and smooth out the top with a spatula.

STEP 3
Place the cake pan in the air fryer basket and air fry at 160°C (320°F) for 20-25 minutes, or until the cheesecake is set around the edges but still slightly jiggly in the center.

STEP 4
Remove the cheesecake from the air fryer and let it cool to room temperature, then refrigerate for at least 4 hours or overnight to firm up. Once chilled, carefully remove the cheesecake from the pan, slice, and serve topped with fresh fruit if desired.

BROCCOLI POPCORN

Cooking Difficulty: 1/10	Cooking Time: 12 minutes	Servings: 2

INGREDIENTS

- 1 head of broccoli
- 1-2 tbsp olive oil
- salt and pepper to taste

DESCRIPTION

STEP 1

Preheat air fryer to 180°C (350°F). Cut broccoli into small florets. Toss broccoli florets with olive oil, salt, and pepper in a bowl.

STEP 2

Spread the seasoned broccoli in a single layer in the air fryer basket. Air fry for 8-10 minutes, shaking the basket halfway through cooking. Once crispy and slightly browned, remove from air fryer and serve immediately.

NUTRITIONAL INFORMATION

Calories: 70, Fat: 5g, Carbs: 6g, Protein: 3g

PEACH WITH CINNAMON DESSERT

Cooking Difficulty: 2/10	Cooking Time: 7 minutes	Servings: 3

INGREDIENTS

- 3 ripe peaches, stoned and quartered
- 1 tbsp. lemon juice
- 1 tsp. cinnamon powder

DESCRIPTION

STEP 1
Preheat air fryer to 360°F. Coat all peaches with cinnamon powder.

STEP 2
Place the peaches in the air fryer cooking basket and cook for 5-7 minutes. Transfer into a serving dish. Drizzle with lemon juice.

STEP 3
Serve and enjoy!

NUTRITIONAL INFORMATION

Calories: 216, Fat: 8.2g, Carbs: 27g, Protein: 9g

AIR FRYER APPLE CRISP

Cooking Difficulty: 2/10	Cooking Time: 24 minutes	Servings: 2

NUTRITIONAL INFORMATION

Calories 460, Fat 36g, Carbs 29g, Protein 8g

INGREDIENTS

- 2 large apples, peeled, cored, and sliced
- 1 tablespoon lemon juice
- 1/2 cup rolled oats
- 1/4 cup almond flour
- 2 tablespoons maple syrup or honey
- 1 tablespoon coconut oil, melted
- 1/2 teaspoon ground cinnamon
- pinch of salt

DESCRIPTION

STEP 1
Preheat your air fryer to 350°F (180°C).

STEP 2
In a bowl, toss the sliced apples with lemon juice to prevent browning. In another bowl, combine the rolled oats, almond flour, maple syrup or honey, melted coconut oil, ground cinnamon, and a pinch of salt. Mix well until everything is evenly coated.

STEP 3
Spread the sliced apples evenly in the air fryer basket. Sprinkle the oat mixture over the apples in the basket.

STEP 4
Place the basket in the air fryer and cook for 15-20 minutes, or until the topping is crisp and golden brown and the apples are tender. Once done, remove the apple crisp from the air fryer and let it cool slightly.

STEP 5
Serve warm, optionally topped with a dollop of coconut whipped cream or a scoop of vanilla ice cream.

CARROT CHIPS

Cooking Difficulty: 1/10   Cooking Time: 17 minutes   Servings: 2

INGREDIENTS

- 2 medium carrots
- 1 tablespoon olive oil
- salt and pepper to taste
- any other spices (such as paprika, garlic powder) optional

DESCRIPTION

STEP 1

Preheat the air fryer to 180°C (350°F). Wash and dry 2 medium carrots, then slice them thinly. Toss the carrot slices with 1 tablespoon of olive oil, salt, and pepper.

STEP 2

Arrange the carrot slices in a single layer in the air fryer basket. Air fry at 180°C (350°F) for 10-15 minutes until golden brown and crispy.Check occasionally and toss if needed for even cooking.

NUTRITIONAL INFORMATION

Calories 50, Fat 3g, Carbs 5g, Protein 1g

CONCLUSION

In conclusion, this cookbook offers a comprehensive guide to embracing the vegetarian lifestyle while utilizing the versatility of an Air Fryer to its fullest potential. By combining the principles of vegetarian cuisine with the innovative cooking techniques of air frying, readers can embark on a culinary journey filled with nutritious and delicious meals.

Throughout the book, we have explored the foundations of vegetarian cooking, emphasizing the importance of plant-based ingredients and the myriad of health benefits associated with this dietary choice. From the principles of preparing vegetarian dishes to the significance of selecting the right ingredients, each chapter provides valuable insights and practical tips for creating wholesome and satisfying meals.

Additionally, our exploration of the Air Fryer has revealed its transformative role in the kitchen, offering a healthier alternative to traditional frying methods without compromising on flavor or texture. With its ability to cook a wide range of foods with minimal oil, the Air Fryer opens up endless possibilities for preparing crispy and delicious dishes, from vegetable chips to protein-packed tofu nuggets.

As we conclude this journey, we hope that readers feel empowered to experiment with new ingredients, techniques, and recipes in their own kitchens. Whether you're a seasoned chef or a novice cook, this cookbook serves as a valuable resource for incorporating more plant-based meals into your diet and harnessing the full potential of your Air Fryer. Here's to embracing a healthier, more sustainable lifestyle through the joy of vegetarian cooking and the convenience of modern kitchen technology.

Stella Harper

Printed in Great Britain
by Amazon

46299907R00079